Ecosystems

Deserts

Greg Reid

CHELSEA CLUBHOUSE

An Imprint of Chelsea House Publishers
A Haights Cross Communications Company
Philadelphia

To Mary-Anne, Julian and Damian

This edition first published in 2004 in the United States of America by Chelsea Clubhouse, a division of Chelsea House Publishers and a subsidiary of Haights Cross Communications.

Chelsea Clubhouse
1974 Sproul Road, Suite 400
Broomall, PA 19008-0914

The Chelsea House world wide web address is www.chelseahouse.com

Library of Congress Cataloging-in-Publication Data Applied for.

ISBN 0-7910-7938-4

First published in 2004 by
MACMILLAN EDUCATION AUSTRALIA PTY LTD
627 Chapel Street, South Yarra, Australia, 3141

Associated companies and representatives throughout the world.

Copyright © Greg Reid 2004

Copyright in photographs © individual photographers as credited

Edited by Anna Fern and Miriana Dasovic
Text and cover design by Polar Design
Illustrations and maps by Alan Laver, Shelly Communications
Photo research by Legend Images

Printed in China

Acknowledgments

The author and publisher are grateful to the following for permission to reproduce copyright material:

Cover photograph: an oryx in the Namib Desert, courtesy of Digital Vision.

John Cancalosi/Auscape International, pp. 15 (top center & right), 15 (bottom right); Jean-Paul Ferrero/Auscape International, p. 23; G. Harold/Auscape International, p. 25; Michael Jensen/Auscape International, p. 27; Oxford Scientific Films/Auscape International, p. 24; John Shaw/Auscape International, p. 18; Voltchev/UNEP – Still Pictures/Auscape International, p. 21; Australian Picture Library/Corbis, pp. 19 (bottom), 22 (inset); Corbis Digital Stock, p. 11; Digital Vision, pp. 3 (top), 8, 9 (both), 12, 16, 17 (top left), 30 (right); Getty Images/Image Bank, pp. 19 (top left & right), 28; Getty Images/Taxi, p. 20; Wade Hughes/Lochman Transparencies, p. 13; Jiri Lochman/Lochman Transparencies, p. 6; Marie Lochman/Lochman Transparencies, p. 7; Photodisc, pp. 3 (center & bottom), 5, 15 (top left & bottom left), 17 (top right & bottom), 26, 29, 30 (left), 31, 32; PhotoEssentials, p. 10; The G.R. "Dick" Roberts Photo Library, pp. 14, 22 (main).

While every care has been taken to trace and acknowledge copyright, the publisher tenders their apologies for any accidental infringement where copyright has proved untraceable. Where the attempt has been unsuccessful, the publisher welcomes information that would redress the situation.

Please note
At the time of printing, the Internet addresses appearing in this book were correct. Owing to the dynamic nature of the Internet, however, we cannot guarantee that all these addresses will remain correct.

The author would like to thank Anatta Abrahams, Janine Hanna, Eulalie O'Keefe, Kerry Regan, Marcia Reid.

Contents

When a word is printed in **bold**, you can look up its meaning in the Glossary on page 31.

What Are Deserts?

A desert environment is part of an ecosystem. An ecosystem is made up of living plants and animals and their non-living environment of air, water, energy, and nutrients.

Most people think deserts are hot, dry, sandy places with no plants. Some deserts are like this, but other deserts have rocky soil with lots of strange plants such as cacti. Some deserts are even made up of ice and frozen earth. What makes a desert different from other places is lack of moisture that plants can use. People also call deserts arid lands or dry lands.

Deserts cover nearly 30 percent of Earth's land surface. They are found on every continent except Europe. Australia is the driest continent—about 70 percent of Australia is desert. The Antarctic and the Arctic regions are sometimes called cold deserts because plants and animals cannot use the water in the ice and snow.

Most deserts are found around the Tropic of Cancer and the Tropic of Capricorn.

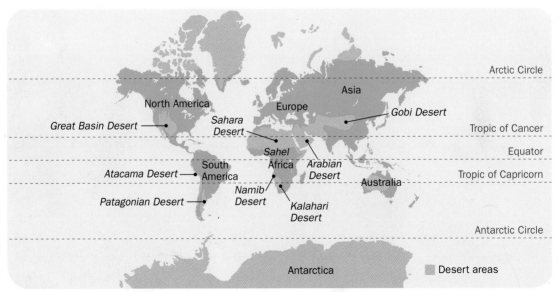

4

Where Are Deserts Found?

Most deserts are close to the Tropic of Cancer and the Tropic of Capricorn. Many deserts lie in the centers of continents. These areas are dry because most rain falls near the coasts. Some deserts are found on the coast. In these areas, cold ocean currents run next to the coast. Less water **evaporates**, so the winds blowing over land do not carry much moisture.

Some deserts lie behind large mountains. Clouds drop their rain on mountains and have very little rain left when they reach the other side. The dry area behind mountains is called a **rainshadow**.

Largest deserts on each continent

Africa	Sahara Desert	3,320,000 square miles (8,600,000 square kilometers)
Asia	Arabian Desert	900,000 square miles (2,300,000 square kilometers)
South America	Patagonian Desert	260,000 square miles (673,000 square kilometers)
Australia	Great Victoria Desert	250,000 square miles (647,000 square kilometers)
North America	Great Basin Desert	190,000 square miles (492,000 square kilometers)

The Largest Desert

The Sahara Desert is the largest in the world.

- Area: 3.32 million square miles (8.6 million square kilometers)
- Length (east to west): 3,200 miles (5,150 kilometers)
- Width (north to south): 1,677 miles (2,700 kilometers)
- Size: covers 25 percent of Africa.

Sand dunes in the Sahara Desert, in Africa

Climate

The desert climate is extreme. The air is very dry. Most deserts have less than 10 inches (250 millimeters) of rain a year, although some have up to 20 inches (500 millimeters). The amount of rain varies from year to year. In some years, no rain falls. In other years, a large amount of rain may fall at once.

Deserts close to the Equator are hot, while those further away are cooler. Some deserts are found in high places. These deserts are cold in winter and warm to hot in summer. Wind storms are common in some deserts.

A dry creek bed in the Little Sandy Desert, Western Australia

Ecofact

Rainless Desert

The Atacama Desert in South America is the only rainless desert on Earth. However, it does receive moisture from fog. Also, every 100 years or so, a rainstorm may drop some rain on a small area.

Seasonal and Daily Variations

Deserts in different places have different seasons and patterns of rainfall. Some deserts have rain in one season. Others get rain throughout the year. Some deserts get rainstorms and others do not.

In deserts near the sea, there is only a small difference between the highest and lowest temperatures in a day. The difference between night and day temperatures in inland deserts is much larger.

Deserts have no cloud cover. The days can be very hot because of the direct sunlight. The nights can be freezing because there are no clouds to hold the heat from the land and the air. In some deserts, dew sometimes forms as the temperature drops at night.

This desert plant gets the water it needs from droplets of dew.

Ecofact

Hot, Hot, Hot

The highest shade temperature ever recorded is 136 degrees Fahrenheit (57.7 degrees Celsius) in the Sahara Desert, at Al Azuziyah, in Libya.

Desert Plants and Animals

Desert plants and animals have many **adaptations** to help them survive. They must all use water carefully and avoid getting too hot or too cold.

Desert Plants

Desert plants grow far apart, because there is not much moisture. Some plants have wide, shallow roots to catch rain. Other plants, such as date palms, have long **tap roots** to get water from deep underground.

Leaves are usually small, thick, and waxy to prevent water loss. Some plants lose their leaves in dry times so the plant can survive. Plants such as cacti store water in their thick stems. They have spines instead of leaves to protect them from being eaten by animals. Many cacti also have a round shape to help reduce water loss. Less moisture is lost when half the plant is shaded from the Sun.

Ecofact

Desert Wildflowers

In some deserts, wildflowers bloom for a short time after rain. They grow quickly and set many seeds before dying. These seeds lie in the soil waiting for the next rain.

The saguaro cactus (*Cereus cactus*) of North America can live for more than 200 years and grow to more than 40 feet (12 meters) in height. More than 80 percent of the plant is water stored in its stem.

Desert Animals

There are many **species** of insects, spiders, reptiles, birds, and mammals in deserts. Because there is not enough water or food, few large animals live in deserts. Animals are usually small and pale in color. This is good for **camouflage** against the light colors of the desert. The pale color also helps to keep them cool by reflecting the Sun's heat.

Animals have also adapted their feeding habits to live in deserts. Most birds such as sandgrouse, reptiles such as desert tortoises, and lizards such as the thorny devil feed during the day. Many animals such as desert hedgehogs and the sand rats of North Africa are **nocturnal**. They hunt at night when it is cooler and live in burrows during the day.

Stinging Scorpions

Scorpions are carnivores (meat-eaters) that hunt at night for insects and spiders. They shelter under rocks or in underground burrows during the day. There are more than 2,000 types of scorpions in deserts around the world. The largest is 6.3 inches (16 centimeters) long.

A desert hairy scorpion

The thorny devil, from Australia, has sharp scales to protect it from **predators**.

Types of Deserts

There are four main types of deserts—hot deserts, semi-deserts, coastal deserts, and cold deserts. Each type of desert is found in different parts of the world.

Hot deserts are found around the Tropic of Capricorn and the Tropic of Cancer.

Semi-deserts are usually found around other deserts and are not as dry.

Coastal deserts have cold ocean currents offshore. These deserts are mainly found on the west coasts of continents. The air blowing over these deserts does not have much moisture.

Cold deserts are found further from the Equator and in the centers of continents. They are also found in some high, inland areas.

A mountain cactus growing in a cold desert in Peru, South America

What Do Deserts Look Like?

Only 15 percent of the world's deserts are made of sand dunes. Most deserts have steep mountains, gravel plains and gravel slopes at the edge of mountains, and dry salt lakes.

Each desert has a different make-up. In the United States, deserts consist of about 2 percent sand dunes and more than 31 percent gravel slopes. The Sahara Desert is made up of about 25 percent sand dunes and only 2 percent gravel slopes. Australian deserts have large areas of dry salt lakes. In the United States, there are many canyons in deserts, including the Grand Canyon.

Ecofact

Low Salt Lakes

The Dead Sea, in the Middle East, is 1,303.5 feet (395 meters) below sea level. It is the lowest point on Earth. Lake Eyre is 49.5 feet (15 meters) below sea level and it is the lowest point in Australia.

The **mesas** and **buttes** in the Monument National Park in Arizona were formed by wind and water taking the sand and rocks away over thousands of years.

Hot Deserts

About 20 percent of the world's deserts are hot deserts. Because these deserts are near the Tropics, they are warmer than other deserts. Day temperatures in these deserts can reach more than 100 degrees Fahrenheit (38 degrees Celsius). The Sun quickly evaporates any moisture in hot deserts. Nights are often freezing cold, as the heat in the air and the ground is lost. Plants and animals in hot desert need special adaptations to survive these extremes of temperature.

Hot deserts include the Mojave and Sonoran deserts of North America, the Arabian and Thar deserts of Asia, the Sahara and Kalahari deserts of Africa, and the Great Sandy and Simpson deserts of Australia. South America has no hot deserts.

Organ pipe cactus in the desert of Arizona

Animal Adaptations

Hot-desert animals have made special adaptations to help them survive the heat and lack of water. Many hot-desert animals, such as bilbies, camel spiders, and fat-tailed rats, are nocturnal. They spend the day in underground burrows to avoid the heat. Sand vipers from the Sahara Desert and the Middle East bury themselves in sand to escape the heat. Nocturnal animals come out in the cool of the night to feed.

Fennec foxes and desert hares have huge ears to help them lose heat and stay cool. Many hot-desert animals do not drink water. Instead, they get their water from the animals and plants they eat. Their **urine** contains little water. Lizards such as the gila monster store fat in their tails. They can go for long periods without eating.

Desert Frogs

In hot deserts, many frogs such as the water-holding frog of Australia and the spadefoot toad of North America spend months or years underground. There they wait for rain to make pools so they can breed.

The Fennec fox is the smallest of all the types of foxes. It has huge ears to help it lose heat and stay cool.

Semi-Deserts

Semi-deserts lie between deserts and grasslands. They get between 10 and 20 inches (250 and 500 millimeters) of rain per year. Rainfall is not reliable or regular and there is a long dry season. There are also periods without rain called **droughts**.

Semi-desert plants have made many adaptations. Many plants, such as acacias, have thorns to protect themselves from being eaten. Shrubs, such as the creosote bush and sage bush, have leaves that are light in color and glossy, to reflect the Sun's heat. These plants often have an unpleasant taste and smell.

A type of creosote plant called black bush in south-east Arizona

Food Chains

Food chains show the feeding relationship between plants and animals. A food chain starts with the Sun, water, and nutrients from the soil and decomposing plant and animal matter. These basic elements supply energy for plants. The next link in the chain occurs when herbivores and omnivores eat the plants. Herbivores eat only plants, while omnivores eat plants and other animals.

A food chain might continue with carnivores. These animals only eat meat. Carnivores are at the top of the food chain. When any plant or animal in the chain dies, **decomposers**, such as worms and bacteria, break down the matter. The decomposed material returns to the soil where plants take up the nutrients to grow, and the cycle continues.

Desert plants, such as mesquite, cat claw, and brittle bushes, get their energy from the Sun and nutrients from decaying matter and the soil.

1 →

Kangaroo rat (herbivore) eats the seeds of these plants.

2 →

3 ↓

Diamondback rattlesnake (carnivore) eats the kangaroo rat.

Semi-desert food chain in North America

7 Plants take up soil nutrients to grow.

↑

6 Red-tailed hawk dies and is decomposed by fungi and bacteria. The nutrients are returned to the soil.

5

Red-tailed hawk (carnivore) eats the roadrunner.

← **4**

Roadrunner (carnivore) eats the diamondback rattlesnake.

Coastal Deserts

Coastal deserts have cold ocean currents offshore. These deserts lie on the west coasts of continents. Coastal deserts include the Namib Desert of Africa, the Atacama Desert of South America, and the Baja California Desert of Mexico.

Summers in coastal deserts are warm and long, with temperatures from 55 to 75 degrees Fahrenheit (13 to 24 degrees Celsius). Winters are cool, with temperatures of around 41 degrees Fahrenheit (5 degrees Celsuis) or less at night. In most years, there is only 3 to 5 inches (80 to 130 millimeters) of rain. Often, no rain falls for many years. Fog is common at night, and it provides coastal desert plants and animals with water.

Ecofact

Ancient Fog Catcher

The welwitschia plant in the Namib Desert is really a dwarf tree. Its leaves have large pores to soak up water from nighttime fogs. The plant lives for more than 1,000 years.

The Namib Desert in Africa

Coastal Desert Food Chain

Many plants and animals in coastal deserts are connected in food chains. They depend on each other for food and nutrients. Here is an example of a food chain from the Namib Desert in southern Africa.

Namib Desert grass (producer) gets its energy from the Sun and nutrients from decaying matter and the soil.

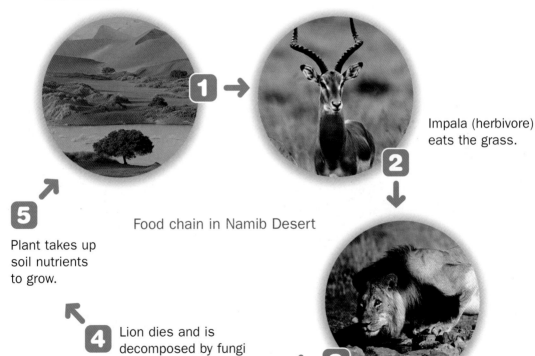

Food chain in Namib Desert

Impala (herbivore) eats the grass.

Plant takes up soil nutrients to grow.

Lion dies and is decomposed by fungi and bacteria. The nutrients are returned to the soil.

Lion (carnivore) eats the impala.

17

Cold Deserts

Cold deserts are found a long way from the Equator. They are also found in the centers of continents and in high places behind mountains. Examples include the Gobi and Iranian deserts of Asia, and the Great Basin Desert of the United States. Africa and Australia do not have any cold deserts.

Winters are cold, with snow and ice. Summers are warm to hot, but nights are cold. Animals need thick fur to keep warm. The main plants are deciduous. They lose their leaves in winter, when the ground is covered in snow and ice. Many plants also have spiny leaves to resist the cold.

Snow in the desert of Arches National Park in Utah

Cold Desert Food Chain

Many plants and animals in cold deserts are connected in food chains. Here is an example of a food chain from the Gobi Desert in central Asia.

Gobi Desert grass or shrub (producer) gets its energy from the Sun and nutrients from decaying matter and the soil.

Food chain in Gobi Desert

Young camel (herbivore) eats grass.

5 Plant takes up soil nutrients.

4 Wolf dies and is decomposed by fungi and bacteria. The nutrients are returned to the soil.

3 Wolf (carnivore) eats young camel (herbivore).

Indigenous Peoples

Indigenous peoples, such as Aboriginal peoples from Australia, and the San (Bushmen) from southern Africa, once hunted animals and gathered food in deserts. Today, very few indigenous peoples live like this.

In African and Asian deserts, **nomads**, such as the Bedouin and Khalkha Mongols, live off the milk and meat from their herds of sheep, goats, horses, and camels. The animals graze on plants before they are moved to another area. Bedouins live in tents, and Khalkha Mongols live in **yurts**. The houses can be packed up quickly when the animals are moved to new grazing areas.

Indigenous desert peoples

Region	Indigenous Peoples	States/Countries Where They Live Today
Africa	Tuareg and Berber (Sahara) San (Bushmen of the Kalahari) Beduoin (north Africa)	Niger, Chad, Botswana, Namibia Egypt, Libya
Asia	Bedouin and Khalkha Mongols	Saudi Arabia, Jordan, Mongolia
Australia	Aboriginal peoples	Australia
North America	Zuni and Hopi Native Americans	United States, Mexico
South America	Incas	Peru, Chile

A Bedouin camp

Desert Farmers

Farming in deserts depends on getting enough water to the crops. Humans grew the first crops along desert rivers. Deserts **oases** are fertile places with natural water springs. Crops of fruit and vegetables grow well. Date palms are valuable oasis trees in some deserts.

Irrigation is used in many desert areas to water crops. Water comes from rivers or wells. Many large rivers—such as the Nile, Tigris, Euphrates, and the Indus—flow through deserts. Some farmers plant crops on the edge of deserts where there is more rainfall. The crops sometimes fail because of droughts. Deserts can bloom if a regular water supply can be found.

An oasis in the Sahara Desert, in Libya

A Valuable Desert Crop: Date Palms

Date palms are valuable trees. They can resist drought and grow in salty soils. Date palms provide fruit, timber for building, and firewood. Their leaves are used for animal feed, roofing material, basket weaving, and making rope.

Desert Resources

Some deserts are rich in natural resources. Salt has been mined from deserts for thousands of years. Oil and natural gas are found in the rocks under some deserts. Middle Eastern desert countries have 65 percent of the world's known oil resources.

Ecofact
Ancient Sharks

The world's largest phosphate mine is located on the edge of the Sahara Desert, at Khouribga, in Morocco. Phosphate is a mineral that comes from animal droppings and ancient sea life, such as sharks. It is used to make fertilizers.

Deserts in Chile and the United States have large copper mines. The Sahara Desert has large iron ore and phosphate mines. Southern African and Australian deserts contain gold and diamonds. In Australia, opal mining occurs in desert areas. The Namib Desert coast is the world's greatest source of gemstones. Solar energy is used to make electricity in the Mojave Desert of California.

A copper mine in Arizona

Ecofact
Pink Diamonds

The Argyle Diamond mine, in the deserts of Western Australia, is the world's biggest diamond mine. Rare and valuable pink diamonds, as well as fine whites and red diamonds are mined.

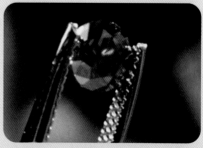

A pink Argyle diamond

Useful Animals and Plants

Some domesticated animals came from deserts. These include camels, Arab horses, ostriches, sheep and goats, **salukis** from Asia and Africa, and llamas and alpacas from South America. Most of these animals are raised for transportation, food, or wool. People keep salukis as pets.

Desert plants such as cacti are popular garden plants. Aloe vera cactus is grown for its sap. The Mexican agave plant is grown for its fiber, which is used to make ropes. Its sweet sap is made into drinks. The jojoba plant from North America is grown for its oil. Scientists believe many other useful desert plants are yet to be discovered.

An agave plantation in Mexico. The fibers from these plants are made into sisal rope.

Ecofact

Camels: Ships of the Desert

There are two types of camels. Dromedary camels from Middle Eastern countries have one hump, and Bactrian camels from the Gobi Desert have two humps. Camels are well adapted to desert life. They can go for a long time without water and have broad, padded feet for walking in sand. Camels have been used to carry people through deserts for more than 4,000 years. Camels originally came from North America, but they no longer live there.

Threats to Deserts

Many countries with deserts are poor and have growing populations. About one-third of the world's deserts are under threat from human actions. Desert lands are coming under pressure from larger herds of grazing animals and more land being cleared for crops. Other threats to deserts include pollution from mining and nuclear waste disposal, dams, defense and weapons testing, wars, and fires.

The largest area under threat is the semi-desert south of the Sahara Desert called the Sahel. The number of domesticated animals in this area increased as wells were built in the 1950s to provide a regular supply of water. Many nomadic people settled down instead of moving around with their herds of animals. The overgrazed areas of semi-desert were not able to grow back and the Sahara Desert grew.

Ecofact

Gulf War Pollution

Pollution from the 1991 Gulf War spread to many desert areas outside Kuwait. Burning oil wells, oil spills, and the destruction of chemical and biological weapons all caused serious pollution.

An oil fire in Kuwait during the 1991 Gulf War

Threatened Plants and Animals

Many desert plants and animals are threatened by human actions such as collecting and hunting. People have also introduced plants and animals from other countries into desert areas. These can sometimes take over the **habitat** of the native desert plants and animals.

In Australia, six desert **marsupials** have become extinct in the past 200 years. Grazing animals, such as cattle and sheep, have changed the habitats of many Australian desert plants and animals. Cats, foxes, and rabbits have also invaded the deserts. Rabbits compete with native animals for food and water, while cats and foxes hunt and kill them.

The Australian bilby is an endangered desert dweller.

Effects of Human Activities on Deserts

About 13 percent of the world's people live in desert areas. The biggest problems are lack of water, droughts, and growing populations. People are pumping **groundwater** faster and deeper than ever before, mainly to irrigate crops. If the water runs out, crops will die and people may starve.

In some areas, salt water has come into the groundwater and soils, making them useless. **Salinity** kills crops and is a serious problem in some deserts. Half of the irrigated land in Iraq has salinity problems. People need to manage deserts carefully or they will not be able to live there.

Too much salt kills plant life.

The Aral Sea: the Shrinking Sea

The Aral Sea, in Asia, was the world's fourth largest lake. People took the water from two rivers that flowed into the sea to use for growing cotton. Today, the sea is very small and salty. Twenty types of fish are now extinct along with a fishing industry that once provided jobs for 60,000 people.

Desertification

Poor farming practices, growing populations, and regular droughts in many areas have caused deserts to spread. This process is called desertification. Too many animals grazing on desert plants can kill them. Plants help to keep the soil together and stop the wind from blowing it away.

Cutting down trees and shrubs for firewood and building material also helps deserts to spread. When the plants are cleared and the soil is plowed to grow crops, wind can easily blow the soil away. In times of drought, crops fail, animals die, people suffer, and the deserts grow larger. Many people become victims of drought and have to depend on outside help to survive.

A camp in Changara, Mozambique, where people whose lives have been ruined by drought rely on charity to survive.

Protecting Deserts

More laws are needed to protect the special plants and animals that live in deserts from becoming extinct. Many countries have set up desert national parks and reserves. South Africa and Botswana have combined two older national parks on their border to form Kgalagadi **Transfrontier Park**, a new 14,672-square-mile (3.8-million-hectare) park. The park covers a large area of the Kalahari Desert.

It is also important that people take action to stop the spread of deserts. Scientists have said that deserts are increasing by 39 square miles (100 square kilometers) every day as a result of destructive human activities. People can help protect deserts by reducing the numbers of grazing animals, planting more trees, and using water more carefully.

An oasis in Ningxia Province, China, with crops and trees

Back from the Dead

The Arabian oryx became extinct from the wild in 1979 because of overhunting. Zoos have bred oryx and released them back into protected reserves of its original habitat.

Ecotourism in Deserts

Ecotourism is when visitors pay to see the beauty of a natural ecosystem. People want to visit deserts because they are so different from other areas. Ecotourism does not cause much disturbance to deserts. Desert tours are very popular in the Sahara Desert and the deserts of Australia. Indigenous people can become guides, showing visitors the desert plants and animals. Ecotourism can help protect deserts for the future.

Special places in deserts around the world may also be protected in World Heritage Areas. The United Nations Educational, Scientific and Cultural Organisation (UNESCO) has a list of World Heritage Areas that are of great importance to the world. Some desert areas, such as the Tassili-n-Ajjer National Park in Algeria and the Grand Canyon National Park in the United States, are protected in World Heritage Areas.

Ecofact

Sacred Rock

Uluru, in Central Australia, was listed as a World Heritage Area in 1987. It is the world's largest monolith (single rock) and a sacred site for Aboriginal people who have lived in the desert for more than 30,000 years.

Uluru

How to Save Deserts

We can all work to save deserts. Learn more about the importance of deserts to the world. Join a conservation group and let others know about the threats to deserts and the threats of deserts growing larger. Write to the government and ask them to help save the world's deserts. The governments of rich countries can help poor countries protect their deserts and stop them from spreading.

ecosystems

The following web sites give more information on deserts.

Desert
http://www.enchantedlearning.com/biomes/desert/desert.shtml

Desert
http://mbgnet.mobot.org/sets/desert/index.htm

Deserts
http://www.kidskonnect.com/Desert/DesertHome.html

Deserts
http://www.ucmp.berkeley.edu/glossary/gloss5/biome/deserts.html

Desert biomes
http://curriculum.calstatela.edu/courses/builders/lessons/less/biomes/desert/desert.html

The desert biome
http://oncampus.richmond.edu/academics/as/education/projects/webunits/biomes/desert.html

Glossary

adaptations	changes that help plants and animals survive in an environment
buttes	small, flat-topped hills formed by erosion
camouflage	when an animal's color or shape helps it to blend into the background
decomposers	organisms, such as worms, fungi, and bacteria, that break down plant and animal matter
droughts	times of water shortage that cause stress to plants, animals, and people
evaporates	when water is heated and turns to gas
groundwater	water in rocks and sediment under the ground
habitat	the environment where organisms live
indigenous peoples	groups of people who first lived in a place, whose traditional ways help them to survive in that place
irrigation	a system of pipes or channels that brings water to crops
marsupials	a group of mammals that carry their young in a pouch
mesas	hills with a flat top and steep sides
nocturnal	animals that come out at night to feed
nomads	people who move from place to place
oases	fertile places in a desert with a water supply
predators	animals that hunt and eat other animals
rainshadow	the area behind mountains that gets little rain
salinity	too much salt in soils
salukis	Bedouin hunting dogs
species	types of plants and animals
tap roots	a long root that reaches deep underground looking for water
transfrontier park	a park that spreads across several countries
urine	the waste water from the body
yurts	Mongol tent made of animal skins and wool

Index